W9-BUI-566

FOOTBALL
FOR FUN!

By Kenn Goin

Content Adviser: Ben Mutzabaugh, College Sports Reporter and Editor, Washington, D.C.
Reading Adviser: Frances J. Bonacci, Reading Specialist, Cambridge, Massachusetts

COMPASS POINT BOOKS

MINNEAPOLIS, MINNESOTA

Compass Point Books
3109 West 50th Street, #115
Minneapolis, MN 55410

Visit Compass Point Books on the Internet at *www.compasspointbooks.com*
or e-mail your request to *custserv@compasspointbooks.com*

Photographs ©: Mike Powell/Getty Images, front cover (left); Artville, front cover (right), 5, 13 (bottom); Bruce Heinemann/PhotoDisc, front cover (bottom); Jonathan Daniel/Getty Images, 6–7, 39; Doug Pensinger/Getty Images, 8–9, 19, 23; Tom Hauck/Getty Images, 10–11, 38, 42 (bottom right); Corbis Royalty Free, 12; PhotoSpin, 13 (top); Christie K. Silver, 13 (center top & center); Courtesy of Rawlings, 13 (center bottom); PhotoDisc, 14–15, 17, 31, 42 (center & bottom left), 43 (top); Scott Halleran/Getty Images, 15; Eliot Schechter/Getty Images, 20–21; Rick Stewart/Getty Images, 21; Jamie Squire/Getty Images, 24–25, 35; Danny Moloshok/Getty Images, 27, 36–37; Elsa/Getty Images, 28–29; Otto Greule Jr./Getty Images 32–33; Laforet/Getty Images, 40–41; Bud Symes/Getty Images, 43 (center); Carin Krasner/Getty Images 44–45 (bottom); David Nagel/Getty Images 44 (bottom right); David Madison/Getty Images, 45.

Editors: Ryan Blitstein/Bill SMITH STUDIO and Catherine Neitge
Photo Researchers: Christie Silver and Sandra Will/Bill SMITH STUDIO
Designer: Jay Jaffe/Bill SMITH STUDIO

Library of Congress Cataloging-in-Publication Data
Goin, Kenn.
    Football for fun! / by Kenn Goin.
        p. cm. — (Sports for fun)
    Summary: Describes the basic rules, skills, and important people and events in the sport of football.
    Includes bibliographical references (p.   ) and index.
    ISBN 0-7565-0430-9
    1. Football—Juvenile literature. [1. Football.] I. Title. II. Series.
    GV950.7 .G65 2003
    796.332—dc21   2002015121

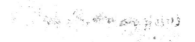

Table of Contents

Ground Rules

Playing the Game

People, Places, and Fun

Note: In this book, there are two kinds of vocabulary words. Football Words to Know are words specific to football. They are in **bold** and are defined on page 46. Other Words to Know are helpful words that aren't related only to football. They are in ***bold and italicized***. These are defined on page 47.

Fall is for Football!

Every fall, people play football games in parks, fields, and stadiums. American football grew out of sports like soccer and rugby. It has its own

set of rules and traditions. While the game is called *foot*ball, players actually use their hands. This book will show you how to play the game the way **professional** teams play it. Start practicing now, and maybe someday you'll make it to the pros.

Goal of the Game

The object of football is to score as many points as possible. Teams also try to hold their **opponents** to as few points as possible. Teams score points by moving the football into the end zone at the far side of the field. The opponent, of course, will try to get in the way.

A football weighs less than a pound (.45 kilograms). It's about 11 inches (28 centimeters) long and 7 inches (18 centimeters) wide at the middle.

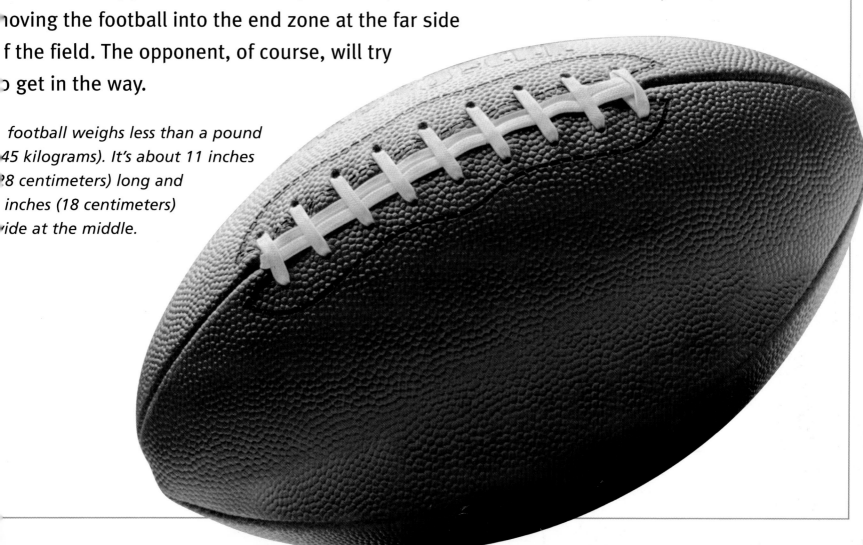

On the Field

Football fields are 120 yards (110 meters) long and 53⅓ yards (49 m) wide. The last 10 yards (9 m) at each end of the field are called **end zones**. **Goalposts** that look like giant yellow slingshots stand in each end zone. The fields are *huge*, but grade school teams play on the same size fields as much-larger adults. Look at the picture to learn the names of the parts of the football field.

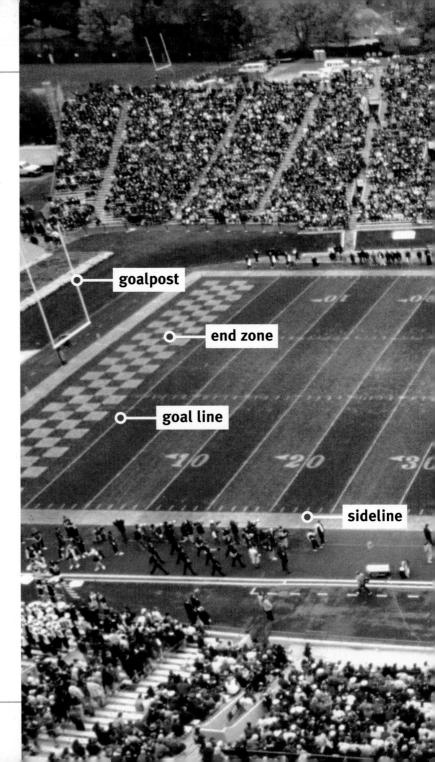

goalpost

end zone

goal line

sideline

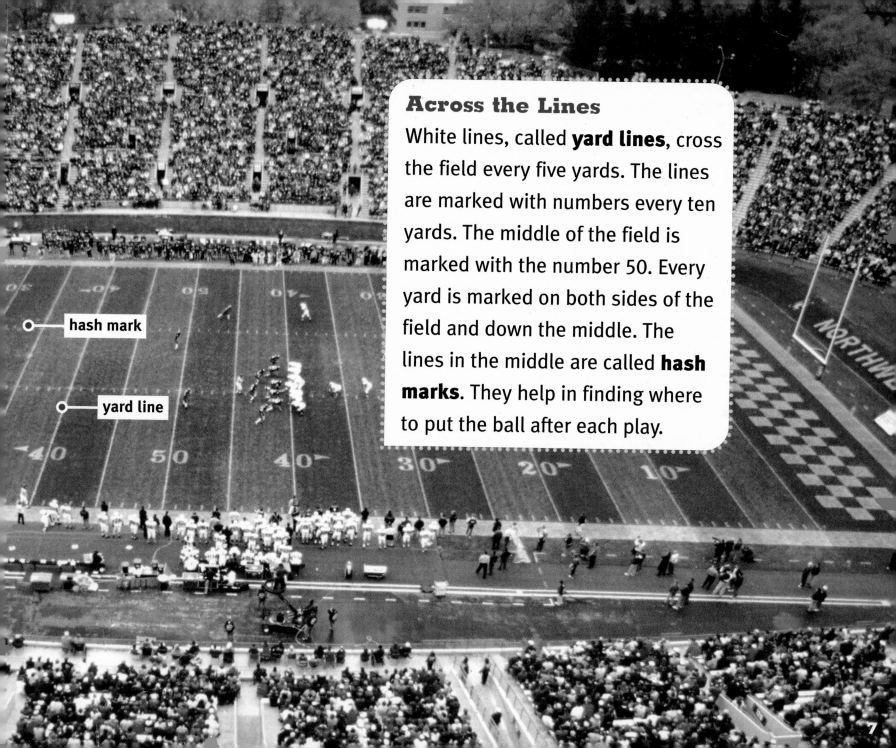

hash mark

yard line

Across the Lines

White lines, called **yard lines**, cross the field every five yards. The lines are marked with numbers every ten yards. The middle of the field is marked with the number 50. Every yard is marked on both sides of the field and down the middle. The lines in the middle are called **hash marks**. They help in finding where to put the ball after each play.

Facing Off

Each team must have eleven players on the field. The **offensive team**, or offense, has possession of the ball. The other team is called the **defensive team**, or defense. Its players are defending their end zone.

Before each **down**, the teams face off along an imaginary line. This is called the **line of scrimmage**. Where is this line? When the ball is placed on the field, the line runs from one side of the field to the other. It runs through the tip of the ball.

line of scrimmage

During a play, the offense tries to move the ball toward the defense's end zone. Players on the defensive team try to **tackle** the offensive player with the ball. To tackle is to knock a player down by grabbing or hitting him or her. While the pros use tackling, many kids' leagues play **touch football**. In this type of football, the defense only has to touch the offensive player to tackle him or her.

Touchdown!

What's the fastest way to score points? Get the ball into the opponent's end zone.

These are the ways the offense can do it:

PLAY	WHAT HAPPENS?	HOW MANY POINTS?
Touchdown	the ball is carried across the goal line	6
Field goal	the ball is kicked through the goalposts	3
Point after touchdown (PAT)	after a touchdown, the ball is kicked through the goalposts	1
Two-point conversion	after a touchdown, the offense carries the ball into the end zone from the two yard-line	2

Oops!
Sometimes the offense is tackled in their own end zone! The defensive team then scores two points. This is called a **safety**.

James Hodgins of the Saint Louis Rams leaps across the goal line for a touchdown.

Get in Gear

When the first football games were played more than one hundred years ago, players wore nothing but their regular clothes. As players have gotten bigger and hit harder, they've needed more and more gear. Today, everyone must wear *protective* equipment.

Modern helmets are made of rock-hard plastic. They have padding on the inside to protect the head. Face guards on the front keep the face safe, too.

A mouthpiece will protect the teeth. It will keep a player from biting his tongue.

Football shoes have cleats on the bottom. Cleats help shoes grip the ground. Players can stop quickly if they have to.

Jerseys (shirts) and pants fit tightly. It is tough for defensive players to grab them and pull a player down during a tackle.

Players also wear padding. When they get hit, it doesn't hurt. Pads are usually worn on the shoulders, knees, and hips.

Start It Up!

Every game begins with a **kickoff**. That's when the ball is kicked into play. The **placekicker** puts the ball in a holder on his or her team's 30-yard line. The placekicker then runs toward the ball and kicks it. At the other end of the field, members of the returning team wait to catch the ball.

The **kick returner** is the player who catches the ball. The kick returner runs toward the opponent's goal line until he or she is tackled. The first set of downs begins where the returner is stopped. Every time a team scores, they have to kick off.

The Coin Toss

Before each game, an official tosses a coin. The visiting team's captain calls heads or tails. If the captain's call is correct, the visiting team chooses whether to kick off or receive. If he or she loses, the home team gets to pick. Teams usually choose to get the ball first.

Down the Field

Every player on the offensive team has a position. Each *position* has a different job to do on each play.

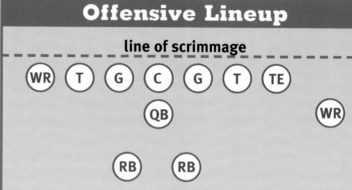

Offensive Lineup

line of scrimmage

WR · T · G · C · G · T · TE

QB · WR

RB · RB

On the Line

• The two guards (G) and two tackles (T) block the defensive players from getting to the quarterback or running backs.

• The center snaps or hikes the ball—throws it between his or her legs—to the quarterback, then blocks.

• One wide receiver (WR), whose main job is to catch passes, stands on one end of the line. (There is a second wide receiver behind the line.)

• The tight end (TE), who blocks and catches passes, stands on the side opposite the wide receiver.

Behind the Line

• Four players stand behind the linemen in the backfield. The quarterback (QB) stands behind the center to receive the ball. He directs the offense on the field.

• The quarterback may hand the ball off to one of the two running backs (RB). Or the quarterback may throw the ball to one of the wide receivers. One of the wide receivers is on the line. The other wide receiver is behind the line.

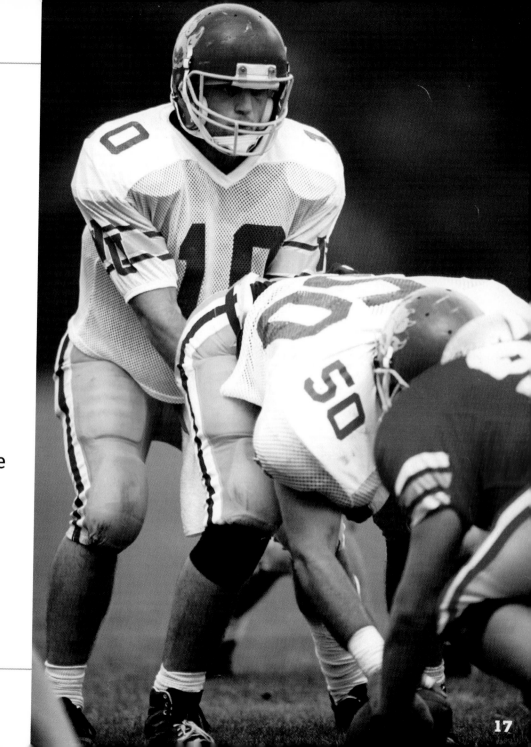

Hold 'em Back!

Every defensive player has one goal in mind: keep the offense from moving the ball and scoring.

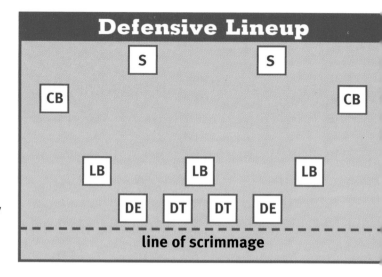

Defensive Lineup

S   S

CB   CB

LB   LB   LB

DE   DT   DT   DE

line of scrimmage

- The **linemen** [two defensive ends (DE) and two defensive tackles (DT)] stand on the line of scrimmage. They are ready to rush forward and tackle the quarterback or running back.

- Linebackers (LB) stand a few yards behind the linemen. They are ready to move forward quickly to stop the ball carrier's movement toward their end zone.

- Cornerbacks (CB) try to block shorter passes that are thrown by the offensive team's quarterback.

- The safeties (S) try to block long passes that the quarterback may throw to a player far down the field.

Get the QB!

When defensive team members tackle the quarterback behind the line of scrimmage, it's called a quarterback sack.

What's a Down?

To understand a football game, you need to know about downs. The offense has four plays—called downs—to move the ball at least ten yards toward its opponent's goal line. If they succeed, they get another set of four downs. This is called getting a first down. If they don't gain ten yards in four downs, the other team gets the ball. If they get close enough to the end zone, the offense can also try to score before it runs out of downs.

How Far?

Q. What does "second and ten" mean?

A. It's the second down. The team must move the ball ten more yards to gain a first down.

Moving the Ball

The offensive team tries to gain yards (move closer to the goal line) on every down. There are two ways to do this—running plays and passing plays.

Running Plays

In running plays, an offensive player runs with the ball. Sometimes, the quarterback hands off the ball to a running back. Other times, the quarterback runs with the ball. The offensive linemen get in front or to the side of the runner. They block the defensive players from tackling him or her.

If a player with the ball drops it or a defensive player knocks it out of his or her hand, it's called a **fumble**. If a player on the defense picks up the ball, the defensive team gains *possession*.

Passing Plays

A quick way to gain yardage is for the quarterback to pass the ball downfield. He or she usually passes to a tight end or wide receiver. If the player catches the ball, the team has a chance of moving many yards before the ball is downed.

If a defensive player catches a pass meant for a receiver, it's called an **interception**. The defensive team takes possession of the ball.

Give It a Spin!

All quarterbacks want to throw the football as far as possible and hit their target. To do this, one must learn how to throw a spiral.

First, grip the ball so the fingers are on the laces. The thumb goes across the seam. Different quarterbacks grip different parts of the laces. Make sure the hand grip is comfortable.

Stand sideways with the foot opposite of the throwing hand closer to the receiver. Bring the throwing arm back. Lean on the back foot. In one motion, swing the throwing arm toward the target and step forward with the front foot. Let go of the ball with the pinkie finger first. Then let go with the ring finger, middle finger, thumb, and finally the index finger.

After the throwing arm follows through, the index finger should be pointing toward the receiver. This should send the ball into a spin toward the receiver's hands.

If you don't get it the first time, that's OK. Keep practicing, and watch the pros.

Something Special

Special teams are somewhere in between offense and defense.

Punts

If it's fourth down with many yards to go for a first down, the offense can **punt**. Punters kick the ball far downfield. The other team is waiting to return it (just like in a kickoff).

Field Goals

Sometimes the offense is too close to the end zone to punt, but not close enough to try for a touchdown. When this happens, they can kick a field goal. The center snaps the ball to the holder (usually a backup quarterback). Then, the kicker tries to send the ball through the goal posts.

Let's Kick It

Here's how to punt. Hold the ball with both hands. Then drop it and kick before it hits the ground. Try to kick it high in the air. This gives the punt a long **hang time**. The bigger the hang time, the better. This gives a team's players more time to run to the other end of the field. They will try to stop the returner. Be careful not to kick too high. If the punt is too high, the ball won't go far enough.

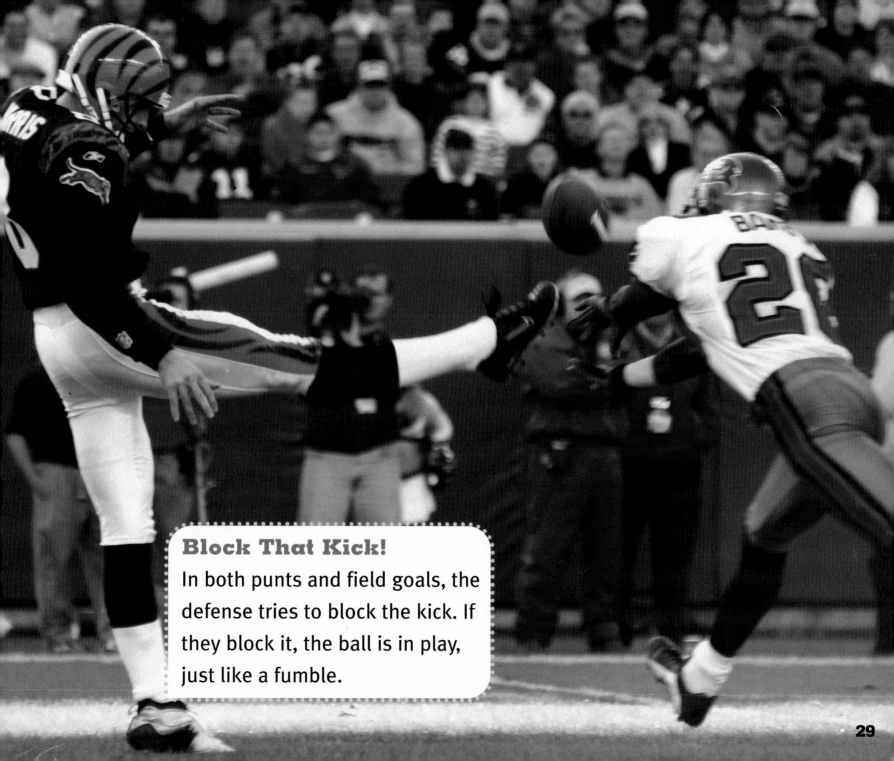

Block That Kick!

In both punts and field goals, the defense tries to block the kick. If they block it, the ball is in play, just like a fumble.

Follow the Rules

Football is a game with many rules. With twenty-two players on the field at a time, there's a lot to keep track of. The rules of the game could fill a whole book. Here are some of the most important ones.

- All football games are played within a time limit. In college and pro football, the ball can be *in play* for no more than sixty minutes.

During the hour of play, the game clock is stopped for many reasons. The most common are: a timeout is called, a score is made, a player is injured, or a player runs out of bounds. That's why games often last 2½ to 3 hours!

When the player with the ball goes out of bounds (over the **sidelines**) or goes down on the field, the ball is out of play. Before the ball goes back in play, it is placed on the hash mark nearest where it went down.

How to Lose Yards

Breaking the rules results in a penalty. This usually gives the other team extra yards or a first down. Game officials watch each play closely. They let everyone know that a rule has been broken by tossing down a flag. When the official announces the penalty, he or she also uses hand signals. There is a hand signal for every penalty in the rulebook.

In the early years of football, there were no penalties. Many of them were added to make the game safer for players.

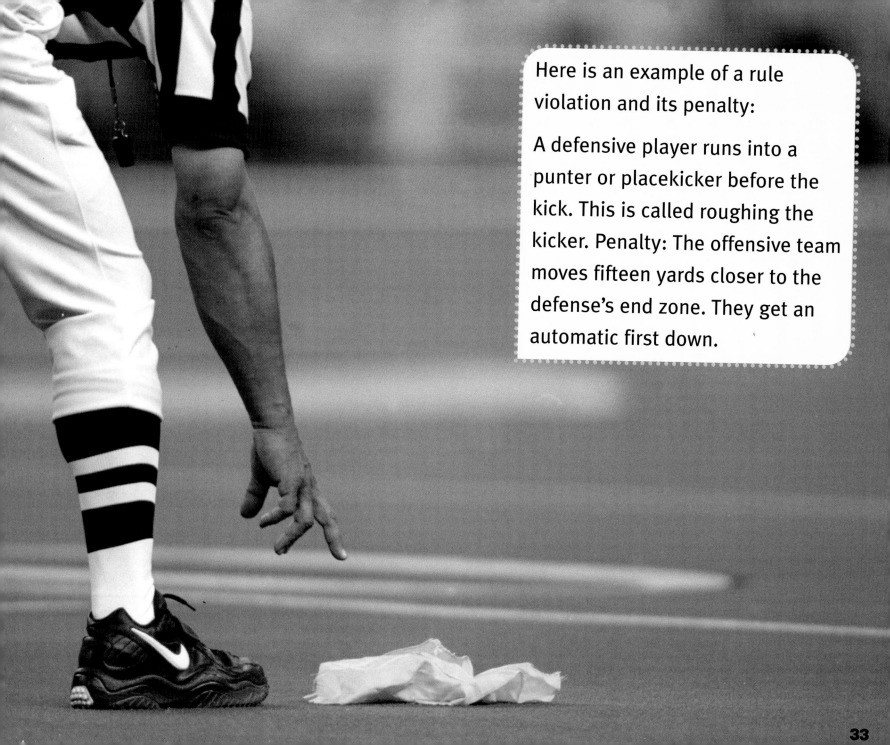

Here is an example of a rule violation and its penalty:

A defensive player runs into a punter or placekicker before the kick. This is called roughing the kicker. Penalty: The offensive team moves fifteen yards closer to the defense's end zone. They get an automatic first down.

Think!

Football is about more than just being big, strong, and fast. There are many positions, plays, and rules. The players on the field need to think. Luckily, the coach and playbook are there to help them.

The coach's job is to **strategize**. The coach must answer questions. Who should the starting quarterback be? Who is the best player to match up against the opponent? What is the best offensive play to call on third and four?

The coaching staffs of college and professional teams also write playbooks. A playbook is a book of plays that teams can use. These include running and passing plays and special teams plays. Defensive formations tell the players where to go and what to do. Playbooks use symbols like Xs, Os, numbers, and lines to explain information.

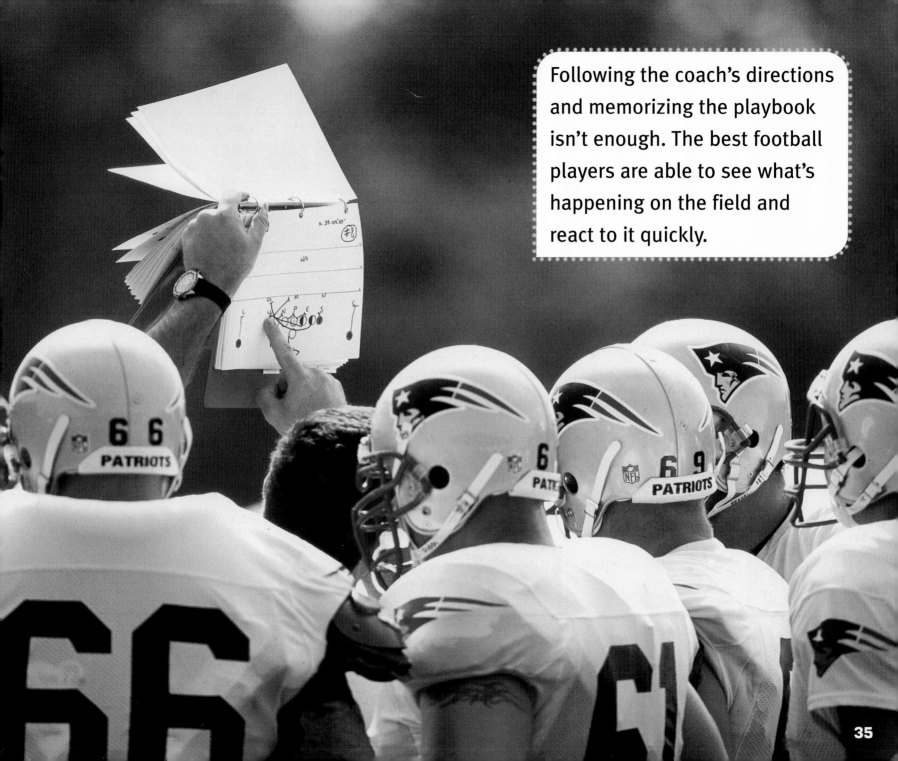

Following the coach's directions and memorizing the playbook isn't enough. The best football players are able to see what's happening on the field and react to it quickly.

The Pros

Colleges were the main place football was played until the 1930s. Today, football is a major sport in middle and high schools as well as colleges. However, the football that's most often seen on television is professional football.

In the early 1900s, only a few football players received money for playing. They usually earned $50 to $250 per game. In 1920, the owners of their teams met in Canton, Ohio. They formed what became the National Football League (**NFL**). Today, the NFL is by far the most popular professional football league. Many fans also enjoy Arena Football League games. Other professional leagues in football history include the Xtreme Football League (XFL) and United States Football League (USFL).

Legends

There are hundreds of great NFL players. Jerry Rice and Dick Butkus are two of the best.

Jerry Rice

Jerry Rice spent most of his career as wide receiver for the San Francisco 49ers. He was born in Starkville, Mississippi, on October 13, 1962. Rice starred at Mississippi Valley State. The 49ers drafted him in the first round in 1985. He holds thirteen NFL records and has had thirteen 1,000-yard seasons. In 1995 he set a record with 1,848 yards in one season. Rice had physical ability, fierce competitive spirit, and a strong work ethic. He was a *dominant* player for more than a decade.

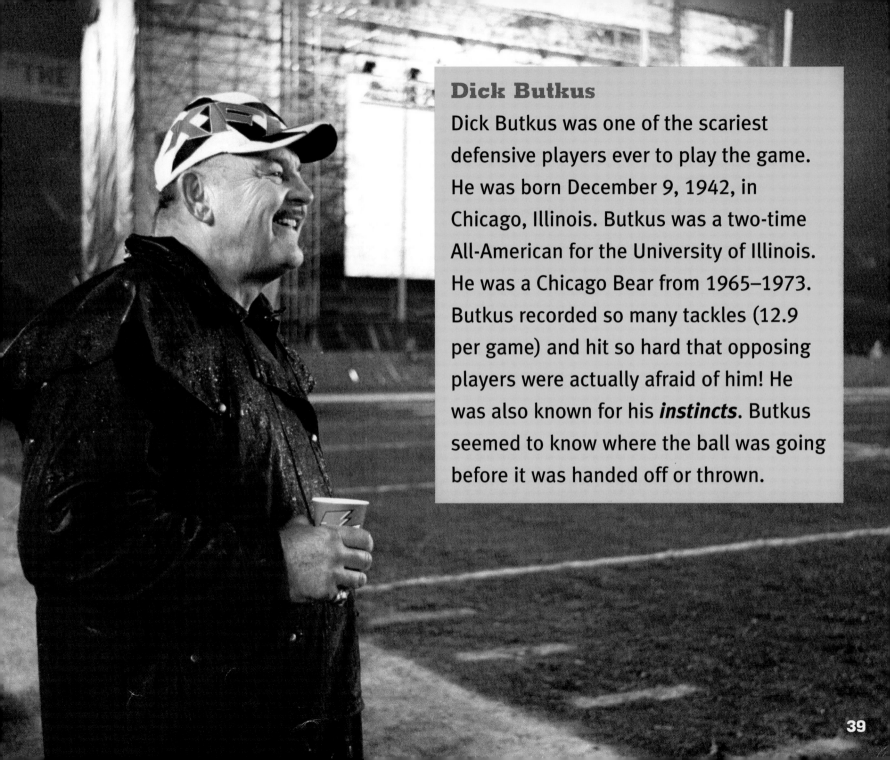

Dick Butkus

Dick Butkus was one of the scariest defensive players ever to play the game. He was born December 9, 1942, in Chicago, Illinois. Butkus was a two-time All-American for the University of Illinois. He was a Chicago Bear from 1965–1973. Butkus recorded so many tackles (12.9 per game) and hit so hard that opposing players were actually afraid of him! He was also known for his *instincts*. Butkus seemed to know where the ball was going before it was handed off or thrown.

The Biggest Game

The NFL includes thirty-two teams, divided into two conferences: the National Football Conference (NFC) and the American Football Conference (AFC). During the first fifty years of professional football, teams from the NFC and AFC (then called the NFL and AFL) almost never played against each other.

Then, on January 15, 1967, the NFL-champion Green Bay Packers played the Kansas City Chiefs, the AFL's best team. Green Bay won. The contest became an annual event, and in 1969, it was named the **Super Bowl**. Today, the Super Bowl is the most watched sporting event on network TV. It is broadcast in ten different languages. All over the world, fans gather to watch the game, the commercials, and the **halftime** show on "Super Bowl Sunday."

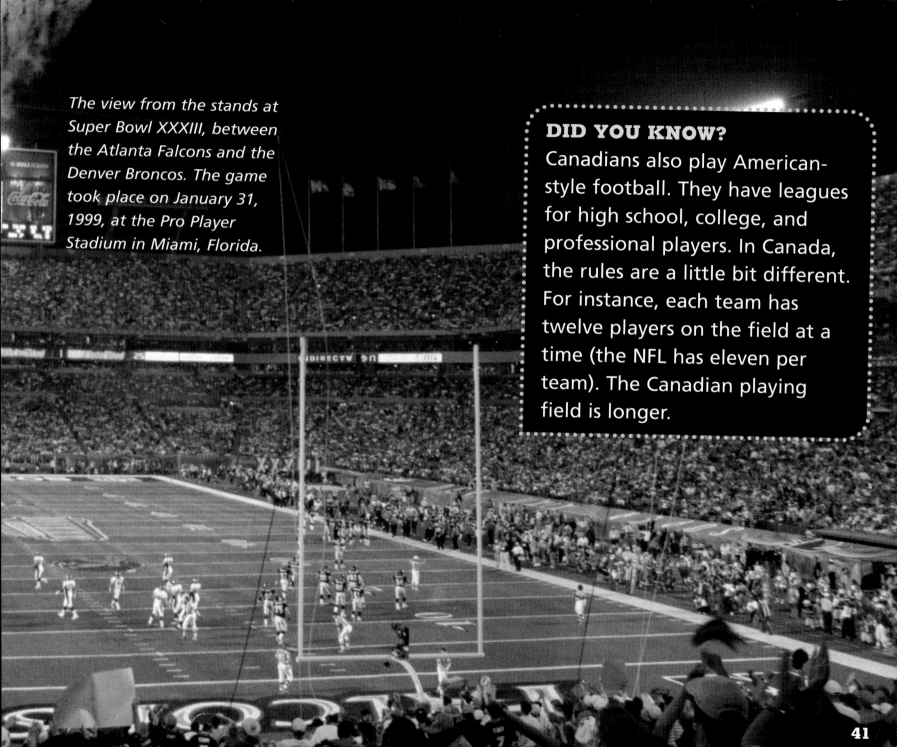

The view from the stands at Super Bowl XXXIII, between the Atlanta Falcons and the Denver Broncos. The game took place on January 31, 1999, at the Pro Player Stadium in Miami, Florida.

DID YOU KNOW?
Canadians also play American-style football. They have leagues for high school, college, and professional players. In Canada, the rules are a little bit different. For instance, each team has twelve players on the field at a time (the NFL has eleven per team). The Canadian playing field is longer.

What Happened When?

1869   1880   1890   1900   1910   1920

1869 First recognized football game is played between Rutgers and Princeton Universities.

1876 Walter Camp, called the Father of American Football, writes first rules for game.

1882 Yard lines are placed across the field at five-yard intervals for the first time.

1888 Tackling is introduced.

1892 Yale University's William Heffelfinger becomes first pro player when he accepts $500 to play for the Allegheny Athletic Association.

1902 First college bowl game is played in Pasadena, California: The Rose Bowl.

1905 Eighteen players die and more than 150 are injured in play, resulting in calls to ban the game.

1914-1916 Fritz Pollard becomes the first African-American player selected for the college All-America Team.

1920 Organization that will become the National Football League (NFL) is formed.

1930   **1940**   **1950**   **1960**   **1970**   **1980**   **1990**   **2000**

1920s Screw-in cleats are first used on shoes.

1939 First NFL game is televised.

1969 First official Super Bowl is held.

1991 The NFL forms the World League of American Football with teams in the U.S. and Europe.

1929 Glenn "Pop" Warner starts what is now the largest youth football league in the world.

1970 NFL begins Monday Night Football.

1994 The two-point conversion becomes legal in the NFL.

1932 First indoor NFL game is played (in Chicago Stadium).

1950s Hard plastic helmets come into wide use.

1985 During the 1985 season, the Bears' William "The Refrigerator" Perry, a 300+ pound defensive lineman, is used as a running back throughout the season and becomes a folk hero.

1997 De La Salle High School in Concord, California, sets a record by winning 100 straight games.

1930s Leather helmets come into wide use.

1954 Wilson Sporting Goods Company becomes the official supplier of balls for all NFL games.

2002 The Houston Texans become the NFL's thirty-second team.

Fun Football Facts

The most points a player has ever scored in one game was 40. Ernie Nevers scored 40 for the Chicago Cardinals, on November 28, 1929.

In the 1920s, the leather football helmets players favored could be folded up and jammed in a pocket!

The first artificial (non-grass) playing surface was developed for Houston's Astrodome. It was called Astroturf.

Most high school games are played on Friday nights. Most college games are played during the day on Saturday. Most NFL games are played on Sundays. This way fans can watch all their favorite games!

There are three men who have kicked seven field goals in one game. They are im Bakken, Rich Karlis, and Chris Boniol.

The average size of an offensive lineman in the NFL has increased 100 pounds (45 kg)! In 1935 234 lb. (106 kg) was the average. Today it is 325 lb. (147 kg).

ootballs are sometimes called pigskins. hey were made of pig ladders filled with air r stuffed straw. Modern ootballs are nade from owhide.

The coldest NFL game ever was played in minus 13 degrees Fahrenheit (minus 25°C). The wind chill was minus 48°F (minus 44°C)! It happened at the 1967 NFL Championship playoff in Green Bay. The Packers beat the Cowboys, 21-17.

Football Words to Know

defensive team: the team that does not have possession of the ball. This team tries to keep the offensive team from getting the ball into their end zone.

down: the period between when the ball is put into play and goes out of play. The offensive team gets four downs to move ten yards toward their opponent's end zone.

end zone: the last ten yards at either end of the field

field goal: when the ball is kicked through the goalposts. It is worth three points.

fumble: when a player drops the ball or it is knocked out of his or her hands by another player

goalposts: the two posts and crossbar that stand in each end zone

halftime: a fifteen minute intermission in the middle of the game

hang time: the amount of time a punted ball stays in the air

hash marks: short lines that mark each yard in the middle of the field

interception: when a defensive player catches a ball meant for an offensive player

kick returner: in a punt or kickoff, the player who catches the ball and runs toward the opponent's goal line

kickoff: the first kick of the game that puts the ball in play

line of scrimmage: the imaginary line along which each team lines up to face off before each down

linemen: the players who stand on the line of scrimmage

NFL: National Football League

offensive team: the team in possession of the ball

point after touchdown (PAT): after the touchdown, the team kicks the ball through the goalposts, scoring one extra point

placekicker: the player who kicks the ball on kickoffs, extra point attempts, and field goals. Placekickers either use a tee or kick the ball while it is being held by a teammate.

punt: a kick that involves dropping the ball and kicking it before it touches the ground

safety: an offensive player is tackled in his or her own end zone, which results in the other team scoring two points.

sidelines: the lines that run down the long sides of the field

Super Bowl: the NFL championship game

tackle: to knock a player down by grabbing or hitting him

touchdown: when the ball is carried into the opponent's end zone; the offensive team scores six points.

touch football: a way of playing the game that does not involve tackling

two-point conversion: when the scoring team moves the ball from the two-yard line into the end zone after a touchdown. It is worth two points.

yard lines: marks made to indicate every yard on the field

Metric Conversion
1 yard = .9144 meters

GLOSSARY
Other Words to Know

Here are definitions of some of the words used in this book:

dominant: very powerful or important

instinct: a way of behaving that a person is born with and does not have to learn

opponent: a member of the team a player is playing against

position: the spot where a player stands on the play, and what the player is supposed to do

possession: when a team controls the ball

professional: a person paid to do a job or play a game

protective: something that makes you more safe so you don't get hurt

strategize: to spend time thinking about ways to do something

Where To Learn More

AT THE LIBRARY

Holden, Steven. *Football: Rushing and Tackling*. New York: Scholastic Library Publishing, 2000.

Lloyd, Bryant. *Football: The Fundamentals*. Vero Beach, Fla.: Rourke Publishing, LLC, 1997.

Patey, R. L., and Patrick T. McRae. *The Illustrated Rules of Football*. Carmel, NY: Ideals Publications, 2001.

ON THE ROAD

Pro Football Hall of Fame
2121 George Halas Drive NW
Canton, OH 44708
330/456-8207
http://www.profootballhof.com

College Football Hall of Fame
111 South St. Joseph Street
South Bend, Indiana 46601
574/235-9999
http://collegefootball.org

ON THE WEB

National Football League
http://www.nfl.com

Arena Football League
http://www.arenafootball.com

National Collegiate Athletic Association Football
http://www.ncaafootball.net

Pop Warner Little Scholars
http://www.popwarner.com/football

INDEX

ABOUT THE AUTHOR

Kenn Goin is a New York City writer and editor specializing in books for kids. He has worked for Macmillan, Golden Books, Scholastic, American Greetings and other publishers. While he usually writes about animals and science, he decided to pen this title to honor the long line of sports fans that he grew up with in Texas and New Mexico.